❖

MILLBROOK ARTS LIBRARY

NATURE
IN ART

by Anthea Peppin

The Millbrook Press
Brookfield, Connecticut

Copyright © 1991 Merlion Publishing Ltd
First published in the United States in 1992 by
The Millbrook Press Inc.
2 Old New Milford Road
Brookfield, Connecticut 06804

Design: Paul Fielder
Series Editor: Charlotte Ryrie

Printed in Spain by Cronion SA

Library of Congress Cataloging-in-Publication Data

Peppin, Anthea
   Nature in art / Anthea Peppin.
      p.   cm. – – (Millbrook arts library)
   Includes index.
   Summary: Examines how various artists depict different parts of
nature in their work and describes some of the techniques used.
   ISBN 1-56294-173-9 (lib. bdg.)
   1. Animals in art – – Juvenile literature. 2. Plants in art –
– Juvenile literature. 3. Nature (Aesthetics) – – Juvenile literature.
[1. Art – – Technique. 2. Art appreciation.] I. Title. II. Title:
Nature in art.   III. Series: Peppin, Anthea. Millbrook arts library.
N7660.P47 1992
704.9'43 – – dc20   91-35014
                                                              CIP
                                                              AC

Cover artwork by Richard Berridge and Gwen and Shirley Tourret
(B L Kearley Ltd); photography by Mike Stannard.

Artwork on pages 9, 13, 20, 23, 28, 33, 38, 41 by Paul Fielder;
pages 7, 15, 37, 40 by Andrew Midgeley and pages 17, 24–25,
30–31 by Edward Russell.

Photographs on pages 5, 9, 10–11, 13, 20, 22–23, 26–27, 28, 33, 38,
41, 42–43 by Mike Stannard.

✤
CONTENTS

Fruit and flowers 4
Wind and water 6
The power of nature 8
Color from nature 10
Warm and cold colors 12
Colors from life 14
Animal patterns 16
Nature from the imagination 18
Let's look at shape 20
Shapes and patterns 22
Mosaics 24
Natural textures 26
Painting texture 28
Designs from nature 30
Block prints 32
Line drawings of animals 34
Painting a special animal 36
Aboriginal bark pictures 38
Totem poles 40
Art materials 42
Artists' biographies 44
Index 46

Fruit and flowers

Some pictures of fruits and flowers look so real that you want to touch and smell them. To get this realistic effect, artists spend a long time arranging and looking at the objects they are going to paint. The finished picture is called a still-life.

The grapes in this still-life look ripe and good to eat. The Dutch artist Jan van Huysum has captured their texture and their color so well that the grapes look real. You can see the gloss on their skins, and you can even make out their seeds where the light is shining through them. Can you see any insects?

Still-life with Fruit and Flowers was painted by the Dutch artist Jan van Huysum.

A year to paint one picture

The date on this painting is 1736–37. This means that the painting took more than a year to finish. The artist was very careful to add every little detail. Because he took so long, his picture shows a mixture of flowers that don't all open at the same time of year.

A pleasing design

The Japanese flower picture was also painted in the 1700s. But it is completely different. The artist, Kitagawa Utamaro, is not trying to make the flowers and insect look real. He is more interested in making a pleasing design on the page. You can count the number of colors that he has used. The picture looks flat, and there is no feeling that the flowers are real.

Paint a still-life picture

You will need paints and a very fine brush. At first, choose something simple to paint. Try painting one or two pieces of fruit and a few flowers.

Balloon-flower with other Plants and Cicada was painted by the Japanese artist, Kitagawa Utamaro.

Spend some time looking carefully at the objects you have chosen. Are they the same color all over? Are they shiny or dull? Is any part of your arrangement in shadow? Mix your colors before you start to paint.

Wind and water

Think of the different kinds of movement you can see in a windy landscape or a stormy sea. Artists have tried many ways of capturing this movement on paper.

Moving water

The Hollow of the Deep Sea Wave was painted by the Japanese artist Hokusai.

The big wave in this picture by the Japanese artist Hokusai looks forceful and full of energy. As the wave rises, a mass of foam is thrown violently from the main body of water. The flying foam looks like fluttering birds being hurled from the wave into the sky.

Hokusai has used different types of line to show the different movements in the wave. He used strong, bold lines to show the force of the wave. He used short, broken lines to show the movement of the foam on the water. In the background is the great mountain Mount Fuji, but the dramatic movement of the sea makes the mountain look tiny and seem unimportant.

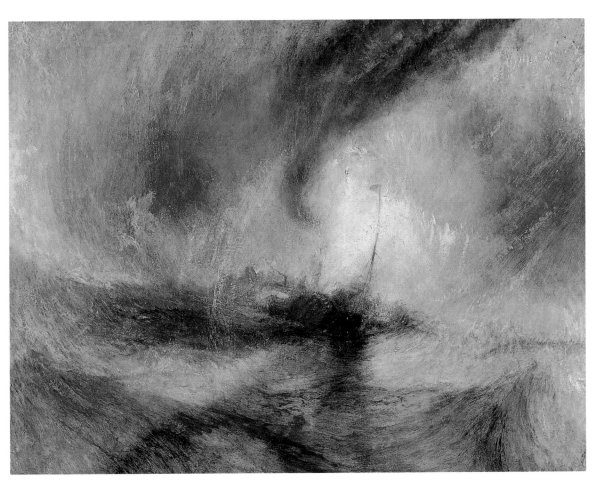

'Snowstorm: Steamboat off a Harbour's Mouth' was painted by the English artist, JMW Turner.

Stormy weather

In the picture on this page, you can almost feel the waves crashing and hear the wind screaming. The English artist Joseph Turner painted the picture after watching the sea in bad weather. He had to be tied to the mast of a ship so that he wouldn't be washed overboard! He was fascinated by the movement he saw in the wind and the water.

Drawing movement in nature

Try to capture movement on paper for yourself by drawing a tree being blown by the wind. First, study a tree bending in the wind. What sort of movement does it make? Is it being blown by a gentle breeze or by a strong gale?

Some movements seem like slow and graceful actions. Others may be violent. You may even see awkward and clumsy movements. Think carefully about what kind of lines you need to make when you are painting different actions.

The power of nature

The Wreck of The Hope was painted by the German artist Caspar-David Friedrich.

When a natural disaster happens today, we often see a film or photograph of it in the news. When the pictures shown here were painted, the artists had to paint a disaster from other people's descriptions.

This picture of a ship caught in icebergs shows us a real event that the German artist Caspar-David Friedrich painted

from his imagination. A ship was sailing in the Arctic Ocean when it became trapped in the ice. The ice froze harder and harder.

As the ice froze, it slowly crushed the ship to pieces. If you look carefully, you can see small pieces of the ship sticking out between great slabs of ice. Do you think the picture is frightening?

Storm collage

You can create an exciting stormy picture with cutout paper. Try to find as many papers with different textures as you can. The idea is to stick down paper shapes to make a special kind of picture, called a collage.

First, make a simple sketch of a storm on a large sheet of paper. Use bold shapes and don't include too much detail. Now decide what colors you want for each part of your picture and then cut out the shapes. Arrange all the pieces carefully on your sketch. Then glue them down. You can add more pieces on top until you are happy with your stormy collage.

Color from nature

People have always wanted to use the colors they see around them in their lives. The earliest people decorated their bodies, their dishes, and their weapons, as well as using different colors in their wall paintings. Today we can walk into a store and buy trays of brilliantly colored paints, which are probably made in a laboratory. But for thousands of years, all colors came from animals, vegetables, or minerals. We call these natural colors pigments.

Some colors can be made from earths that have been tinted with natural materials, such as iron. To be made into paint, these special earths are ground to a fine powder and mixed with something sticky, such as egg yolk or oil.

Precious stones

Some of the brightest colors have always come from stones. It is rare to find much blue paint in early paintings, because the brightest blue, ultramarine, was very expensive. Ultramarine comes from a semiprecious stone called lapis lazuli. The best lapis lazuli has always been found in a mine in northern Afghanistan.

Vermilion is a red pigment and one of the longest-lasting colors. It comes from a rare mineral called cinnabar, which is crushed and ground to a fine powder. Cinnabar was once so precious that the ancient Romans used to transport it from mines in Spain under armed guard.

Colors from animals

Some colors were made from the crushed bodies of animals. Red pigment came from the dried bodies of female cochineal beetles. These beetles were found only in Mexico and South America. This red pigment became available in other countries only after the 1500s, when Europeans brought it from South America. The ancient Romans even made purple from shells.

Colors from plants

Some of the most common paint colors have always come from plants. A deep blue can be made from the crushed leaves of the woad plant, which grows all over southern Europe and Asia. A bright golden yellow, called saffron yellow, comes from crocus flowers. Crushed berries and seeds can also provide bright colors. You can even make yellow from onion skins. Plant dyes such as these tend to fade in sunlight, so they are not often used today.

Poisonous colors

Some colors are poisonous if they are eaten. For thousands of years, painters made a bright yellow called orpiment from the poison arsenic. It is too dangerous to use anymore. A clear white paint can be made from poisonous lead powder. Lead paint is now supplied as thick paste so that you can't breathe in any particles.

Warm and cold colors

The Allotments was painted by the Dutch artist Vincent van Gogh.

What colors do you think of when you think of nature? Do you think of green leaves and grass, or brown earth and branches? Or do you think of blue sky and sea, or yellow sun and sand? It will probably depend on where you live. Can you tell where the pictures on these two pages come from by looking at the colors?

Cool blues and greens

The Dutch artist Vincent van Gogh painted the picture above in the 1900s in France. He mainly used pale blues, greens, and yellows. The painting gives the impression of a cool summer's day in northern France.

Color and movement

Van Gogh was fascinated by the colors he saw in nature. He believed that by painting different colors with short, thick brushstrokes, he could capture the mood of the landscape he was painting. Do you think he succeeded in this painting?

If you look at the sky, you can see how van Gogh used his brush. There are lots of slightly different shades of blue and yellow, painted with swirling brushstrokes. The cool colors make the sky seem restless, as if rain were about to fall.

Warm, golden colors

Do you get a different feeling from this painting? It was painted by an Indian artist named Abul Hasan, who has also chosen colors that blend well together. But whereas van Gogh used a cold blue-green, this artist painted with a warm, golden green. Although nearly all the animals and birds are moving busily, the soft colors make the picture seem warm and peaceful.

Shades of green

Try making warm and cold shades of green. Take some blue paint and some yellow paint, and mix them in a small jar to make green. Paint several broad stripes in the center of a sheet of paper.

Put half of your green into a second jar and mix a little yellow paint into it. Paint a stripe of this new color on the left side of your green stripes. Now mix a little blue into the other jar. Paint a broad stroke of this color on the right side of your original green stripes. Keep adding a little more blue to your blue-green jar,

Squirrels in a Chennar Tree was painted by the Indian artist Abul Husan.

and a little more yellow to the other jar. Every time you change the color, paint a fresh stripe.

Colors from life

Many birds have brightly colored feathers. Some animals have skins with striking patterns. But most animals are simply colored, so that they don't stand out from their surroundings.

A lifelike hare

The Hare was painted by the German artist Albrecht Dürer.

Some artists can make even the dullest colors look interesting. The German artist Albrecht Dürer produced many fine drawings and paintings. He believed that it was important to observe and study animals and nature closely. He often made dozens of sketches of the same creature. This hare is so lifelike that you almost want to pick it up from the paper and stroke it.

Types of paint

Dürer obviously studied the hare extremely carefully before he painted it. How many different shades of brown can you see in the fur? Dürer has colored the hare with two different types of paint. He has used watercolor in some places and gouache in others. Watercolor is a light, see-through type of paint. Gouache is a much thicker paint. Gouache helped Dürer to get a heavier effect than the watercolor, even though he used exactly the same shade of brown.

Realistic colors

The American artist John James Audubon painted more than 400 pictures of North American birds. Audubon has exactly matched the white of this heron's feathers, and the yellow and brown of its legs. Do you find it as appealing as Dürer's hare? Audubon's birds were painted for a book. He wanted to show the accurate colors and details of every bird in North America. He was not interested in making pleasing pictures to hang on a wall.

1502

A Great White Heron was painted by the American artist John James Audubon.

Nature's brighter colors

You can paint a colorful picture from nature to treasure! You will need a watercolor paintbox and a notepad. Go out and look for butterflies on a bright day. They will not stay still long enough for you to paint them, so just make some sketches at first.

Sketch the shape of the butterfly, and mark the patterns on its wings. Put blobs of paint on your sketches to show you what colors to use when

you start painting. If your colors don't look very lifelike, make some notes, too. Later on, use your sketches and notes to guide you. Carefully paint your butterfly.

Animal patterns

This design comes from an ancient British manuscript.

The first books ever made were written by hand. They had beautiful illustrations on nearly every page. Pictures were important because few people could read. The earliest British books, which we call illuminated manuscripts, were made by monks about 1,300 years ago.

The pictures on these two pages come from an early British book called the Lindisfarne Gospels. Strange animal shapes weave in and out of each other. They form a pattern of complicated knots and links. If you look closely, you can trace a single strand of the pattern as it winds its way in and out of all the other strands. This type of page is often called a carpet page.

Copy an animal pattern

Try to copy one of these interweaving animal patterns. Take a sheet of white paper and some brightly colored felt-tip pens. You don't have to use the colors we have shown. Concentrate on copying just one of the animals at first.

When you feel confident, try to make up your own patterns. You can use as many strands of colors as you like. See how complicated your patterns can be! You could join up your patterns to make a colorful border like the one on this page.

Nature from the imagination

A tiger crashes through the jungle. His eyes are opened wide, his teeth are bared in a snarl. His striped tail is curling and lashing against the undergrowth. Lightning is flashing in the distance, and the rain is pouring down.

This sounds like a very frightening scene. But in this painting by the French artist Henri Rousseau there is no feeling of danger. Everything seems still, like a moment from a dream. Rousseau is not trying to show us something that is really happening. He had never visited a jungle, and he may not even have seen a tiger. He is more interested in looking at colors, shapes, and patterns.

Look how the dark green leaves at the bottom of the picture overlap the thin stripes of grass. As your eyes move to the left, the grass shapes become wider and stronger. The pattern that they make partly covers the tiger's stripes.

Painting patterns

Rousseau has painted the grass and leaves in layers, one on top of another. This suggests that the tiger is in the middle of the jungle, behind the leaves. But look at the way the back half of its body is on top of the grass, while the front half is behind. There is no feeling of distance. Everything looks flat. Do you think the tiger looks like a cardboard cutout?

Create a tropical forest

Henri Rousseau worked as a customs officer. Painting pictures was his hobby. Many of his pictures show animals from faraway places. Try painting a picture of a tropical forest for yourself, even if you have never seen one.

Think about the shapes and patterns of leaves and make up some exotic plants. They don't have to be realistic! Mix lots of different greens, yellows, and browns, and then paint different shapes. Your plants could bend and curve as though they are moving in the breeze. Why not add one or two cut out animals?

Tropical Storm with a Tiger was painted by the French artist Henri Rousseau.

Let's look at shape

When we draw, we often start with the outside line of a shape. This is called the outline. You can see the shape of an object more clearly if you cut it out of paper. Try cutting a snail shape from thick paper, without drawing the animal first. In other words, use your scissors instead of a pencil. You don't need to cut the whole shape at once. You could make the shell first, then add the head, neck, and body later. Check that all the pieces fit together, then glue them onto a large sheet of cardboard.

You might like to make a shape collage of a group of animals. Give them an environment to live in, such as a forest or a desert.

This collage by the French artist Henri Matisse is called *The Snail.*

Making a snail out of shapes

The collage above was made by a French artist named Henri Matisse. He began by painting large sheets of paper with bright colors. Then he cut or tore them into shapes. Matisse arranged the shapes very carefully on his background. At first he only pinned them down. When he was happy with the arrangement of shapes and colors, he glued the pieces down.

Matisse called his collage *The Snail.* Look carefully and you will see why. Let your eyes follow the colors, starting with the green in the top corner on the right. The shapes inside the orange border trace a spiral — just like the shape of a snail's shell. Is your animal collage anything like this one by Matisse?

Shapes and patterns

View of Salisbury Cathedral from the Bishop's Grounds was painted by the English artist John Constable.

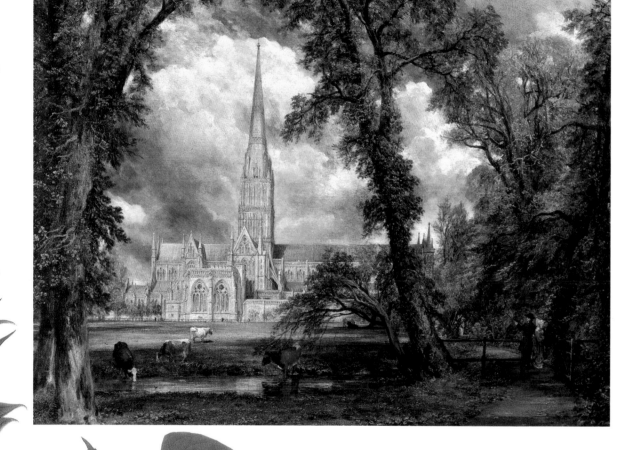

When artists are painting trees and plants, they often concentrate on the shape and pattern of leaves. Some pictures of trees are painted in a realistic way. Other pictures of nature don't look at all real at first.

Realistic leaves

Look at this painting by the English artist John Constable. His trees look solid and real. The painting is almost like a beautifully arranged color photograph. Yet if you look closely, you can see that every leaf is exactly alike.

It would take artists far too long to paint the trees exactly as they are in nature, where every leaf is different. Instead, they copy the shape and pattern of the leaves.

Recognizing shapes

The Swiss artist Paul Klee paints in a completely different way! His trees do not look at all real, but they are easy to recognize. He has painted trees as simple shapes. Some of the shapes curve and bend like graceful young trees. Others are hard and clipped, like tall trees in a city park. Paintings like this look simple at first. In fact, Klee studied the landscape just as carefully as Constable did. Both painters had a great understanding of the patterns found in nature, which they expressed in different ways.

Look at leaf patterns

Make a collection of leaves from plants around you. They will all be different shapes. Some will be long and thin. Some will have jagged edges. Some will be rounded. Look at the patterns on the leaves, too. Are they made of a few strong lines, or many fine lines?

Printing patterns

Choose the leaves that have clear patterns and a strong shape. Paint over the rough side of the leaf with paint. Then press it down on the paper.

Park near L was painted by the Swiss artist Paul Klee.

Mosaics

Mosaics are pictures or patterns made from small pieces of glass, marble, or other stone. Mosaics last for a long time because these materials wear away very slowly. They have been used as wall or floor decorations in different parts of the world for thousands of years.

Roman mosaics

Some beautiful mosaics have been discovered at Pompeii, in Italy. Pompeii was a Roman town that was buried in ash when a volcano called Mount Vesuvius erupted about 2,000 years ago. The Pompeiian mosaic in the picture

This Roman mosaic was discovered at Pompeii, in Italy.

shows marine life that can still be caught in the warm waters of the Mediterranean Sea. Each tiny colored square was chipped by hand from slabs of marble or other stone. The squares were laid one at a time onto a layer of cement.

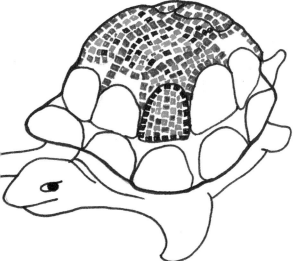

A jigsaw mosaic

Some mosaics were made from large pieces of marble cut into different shapes. These pieces were then fitted together like a jigsaw puzzle. Why not try this method, too? Draw a simple shape of an animal, such as this macaw. Mark different sections on its body. Put your drawing on top of five different-colored sheets of paper.

Cut around each section of your drawing, making sure that you cut through every layer of paper. Then separate all the pieces, and fit them together using a different color for each section. You will be able to make five mosaics.

Make a paper mosaic

You will need sheets of different-colored paper, scissors, and glue. Use one of the sheets of paper as the backing for your mosaic. Decide what animal or plant shape you are going to make. Then sketch its outline on your backing sheet. Cut out lots of squares from your colored papers. Starting in the middle of your picture and working outward, glue each square onto the backing paper. Leave a small gap between each square.

Natural textures

The surface of every object has its own special look and feel. This is called its texture. A log of wood has a rough texture. But the surface of a pebble is smooth. Texture is a very important part of many artists' work.

Textures to touch

Find out more about texture by making a collection of objects with different surfaces. Look for objects made from wood, cloth, metal, and stone. Try to find objects that are hard, soft, smooth, and rough. Put your collection on a table. Now close your eyes and handle each object in turn. Can you recognize the textures of the objects by feeling them?

Looking at texture

We don't always have to touch something to understand its texture. Sometimes we need only to look. The photographs above show four familiar surfaces. We can tell which is cold and hard, and which is rough and knobby, just by looking at them. Our eyes and our memory tell us what to expect.

Magnifying texture

We can use photographs to explore texture in detail. A camera can be used like a magnifying glass. It can show us the tiny details on the surface of a butterfly's wing or a bird's feather. Try looking at your collection of objects through a magnifying glass. What new textures can you discover?

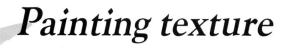

Painting texture

Photographers can take close-up pictures of a surface and show us its texture. But some artists can create textures with paint. They can paint rough wood or soft fur that looks real enough to touch! Here are some ideas for exploring texture yourself.

Mix some thick paints together. Put the mixture onto your paper with quick strokes using a large, dry brush. Try to make a rough, scratchy texture.

Add more water to the paint. Make your paper damp with a wet sponge. Load your brush with paints and drip blobs onto the damp paper. Watch the paint spread out into velvety patches.

Rub a candle or a crayon over a sheet of paper. Now brush paint over the whole sheet. The waxy areas will show through the paint. Find out how many other textures you can make using paint and crayon.

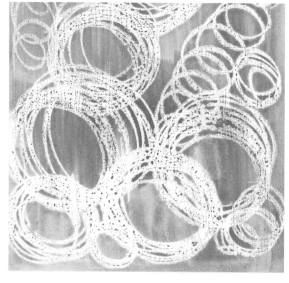

Painting fur

The dog in the picture above was painted by the Flemish artist Jan van Eyck. See how much care he has taken in painting the texture of the dog's fur. Can you imagine how it would feel to touch? The fur at the bottom of the woman's dress looks even softer.

You might like to try making a very careful painting of a texture such as fur or feathers. You could use a magnifying glass to help you see the details — and a small, fine brush to help you paint them.

The Arnolfini Marriage was painted by the Flemish artist Jan van Eyck.

Designs from nature

This tile was designed by the English artist William de Morgan.

The artists who made the pictures on this page have not tried to make them lifelike. They have made patterns to fit particular shapes, and they have used plant and animal forms as the pieces of their patterns.

Animal tiles

The English lizard tile on this page was designed about 100 years ago by an English artist named William de Morgan. You can see how the shape of the animals has been made to fit into the square shape of the tile. Tiles often have the same design in each corner so that they fit together to make a continuous pattern.

Repeating patterns

This picture shows a design for fabric. The design was also created about 100 years ago, by an Englishman named William Morris. He liked to design complicated patterns out of natural curves and shapes.

Look at the way the shapes are carefully placed so that the pattern repeats itself. Do you think the plants and birds look real? Can you find any straight lines in the design? William Morris never used any completely straight lines, because he could find none in nature.

This fabric design by William Morris is called *Strawberry Thief*.

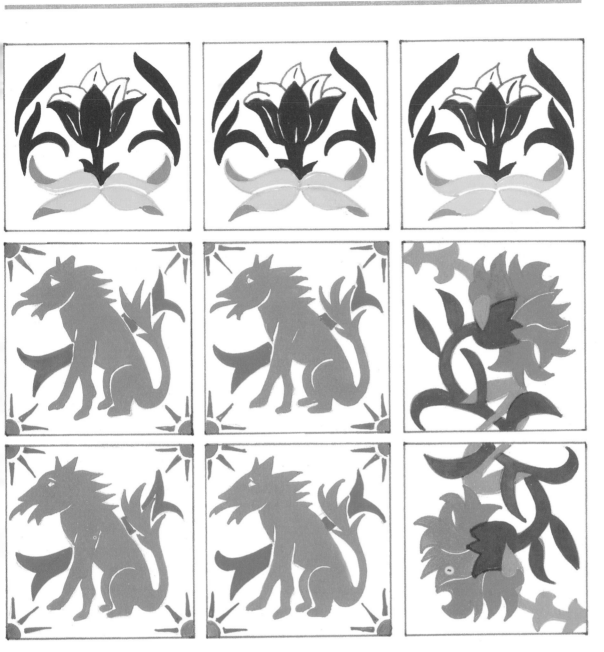

Design a pattern to fit a square

You need a piece of paper about 5 inches (13 centimeters) square and some colored crayons or felt-tip pens. Use plant shapes for your first design. You could copy one of the shapes on these pages. Make your designs twist and curl to fill the square. Then try an animal or bird pattern to fit another square. Make this design as simple as possible.

Draw firm outlines. Don't worry about making the animal look realistic. You are making a flat pattern, not a picture that looks solid. Color all your designs with bright colors.

Try to design a pattern that repeats itself. The easiest way to do this is by placing a simple pattern, such as the one at the bottom of this page, in each corner of one of your squares. Put several squares of the same design together as one pattern.

Block prints

This frog is a print from a woodcut by the Japanese artist Hoji.

This Japanese frog is printed from a woodcut. To make a woodcut, an artist draws a design on a smooth piece of wood. The artist then cuts away all the parts that he or she wants to be white in the print, and leaves untouched the parts that are going to be dark.

To create a single black line, the wood must be cut away from both sides. The bits that are cut out won't catch the ink, so they will stay white. Was this frog's mouth cut out of the wood, or left uncut? Hundreds, even thousands, of prints can be made from one single woodcut before it wears out.

Detailed prints

A woodcut with many fine lines cut into it is called an engraving. This wood engraving of a nightingale was made about 200 years ago. The English artist Thomas Bewick made hundreds of woodcuts like this one to illustrate books about birds and animals. He must have been very patient, for all his engravings are tiny and full of details. Blocks for engravings are usually made from boxwood, which is hard and lasts for a long time.

This nightingale is a print from an engraving by the English artist Thomas Bewick.

Make your own prints

You can make a printing block for a simple animal shape. You don't have to use wood — some clear and simple prints can be made by using a vegetable, such as a potato.

Cut the vegetable in half so that you have a smooth surface. Leave it to dry for a few minutes. Choose a simple animal shape. Cut this shape out of the smooth surface. You will need to use a sharp knife, so make sure there is an adult to help you. Paint thickly over the cut side of the vegetable, but try not to get any paint into the grooves you have cut out. Then print your shape on paper.

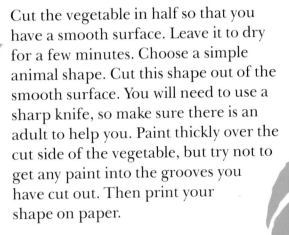

Line drawings of animals

Elephant was drawn by the Dutch artist Rembrandt.

Some of the earliest drawings ever made are pictures of animals. Animals have always been important for food and for work. People have also kept animals in and around their homes for hundreds of years.

A circus animal

Look at this picture of an elephant. With just a few strokes of chalk the Dutch artist Rembrandt has drawn the elephant's shape and its wrinkled skin exactly. Look at the way he uses heavy shading to make the animal seem solid and real.

Rembrandt had probably never seen an elephant before. He drew this one when he saw it in a traveling circus in Holland.

Quick sketches

Artists sometimes make a whole page of quick drawings of animals to show them in different positions. The famous Italian artist Leonardo da Vinci made these sketches of cats — although one of the animals is not a cat at all! He shows us how peaceful cats look when they are curled up asleep, but also how a prowling cat can look as fierce as a lion.

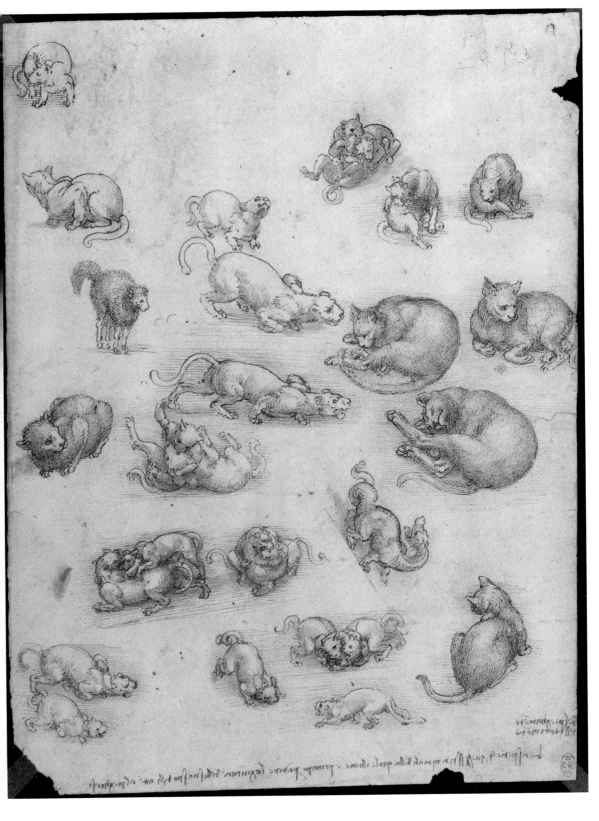

Sketches of Cats was drawn by the Italian artist Leonardo da Vinci.

Draw an animal

Choose an animal that you can study closely. It may be an animal that lives in your house. It could be an animal in a park or a zoo. Draw the outline of the animal you have chosen quickly, without putting in too much detail at first. Notice the way some areas of the animal are in shadow. Shade in these areas on your pictures.

Painting a special animal

Turkey Cock was painted by the Indian artist Mansur.

A rare bird

This turkey was sent from Portugal as a present to an Indian emperor about 350 years ago. Turkeys were very rare in India at that time. The emperor was so pleased with the turkey that he ordered its picture to be painted! The artist, Mansur, has obviously studied the turkey closely, for he has painted lots of tiny details. We can clearly see the patterns and colors on the bird's glossy feathers.

White Ram was painted by an unknown English artist.

When we look at an animal portrait, we can often tell more about the owner of the animal than about the animal itself. Sometimes people simply want a picture of an animal they treasure. Sometimes they want a picture to boast about.

A huge beast

You probably think this ram looks rather unpleasant, but the farmer who owned this large creature was very proud of it. It's hard to see the shape of the ram's body underneath its enormous fleece. Look at how realistic the background landscape looks, compared to the exaggerated figure of the ram.

Make an animal portrait

Choose an animal that is special to you. The ram in the picture was important because it was so fat and had such thick wool. You might choose a dolphin, because it is so graceful, or a cow, because it gives lots of milk. How can you show these things in a picture? Usually artists make an animal look best by painting it from the side.

You need a sheet of paper, a pencil, and some colored pencils. First draw a frame around the edge of the paper to color in later. Then draw your special animal from the side as carefully as you can. When your pencil drawing is finished, decorate the frame with a design to match your animal. Now color your picture. Think about what colors will make your picture as attractive as possible.

Aboriginal bark pictures

This Aboriginal bark painting is called *Dreaming*.

The drawings of Aboriginal people in Northern Australia tell us all sorts of things about their life and their history. Their pictures were usually scratched in the bark of trees, or on rocks and the walls of caves.

Aborigines have always hunted animals and fish and gathered plants and berries for their food. Many of their pictures show animals and hunting scenes. Most of the pictures tell stories. The picture on this page is part of a larger bark painting that tells a story about the birth of one group of Aborigines.

Magic

Sometimes Aborigines drew the insides of an animal as well as its outline. Can you see this in the large picture? The artist wanted to show the inside parts of the animal because they were all important in some way. Some parts were important for food. Others were important because the Aborigines believed they had magical powers.

Make a scratch drawing

You need a sheet of paper, some colored crayons, and a thin, pointed stick. Cover your paper with several stripes of crayon in different colors. Then cover the stripes with a thick layer of one dark color. Using the stick, scratch a simple animal shape, like the Aboriginal ones, into the dark wax. The colors will show through.

This is an Aboriginal bark painting of kangaroos

Totem poles

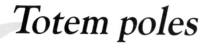

This is a North American Indian totem pole.

A totem pole is a column of wood carved with figures called totems. Each totem has a special meaning. Totem poles are the earliest and best-known examples of the art of North American Indians.

The first totems were images of animals that the Indians believed were their ancestors. Most totem figures represent birds, fish, or other animals. Some are imaginary beasts from ancient stories. The Indians believed that these images would protect them from harm.

You can see only the front of the totem poles in these pictures, but the back would also be carved. Sometimes the images would be brightly painted. On early totem poles, only important parts such as the eyes and ears of the totems were painted.

Types of pole

There were four different kinds of totem pole. Memorial poles were carved to celebrate a special event. House posts were carved poles that formed part of the structure of a building. House-front poles stood against the front of a house, near the entrance. Grave posts were carved poles that supported a box to hold the body of the chief when he died.

Important families

Each family in a tribe had its own totems. If you see a tall totem pole, you know that the family who owned it was important. Some totem poles were 88 feet (27 meters) tall!

Your family totem pole

Choose three animals to carve. They could be animals that are important to your family. Try to make your pole about 12 inches (30 centimeters) tall.

Find a hard, flat surface where you can work. You will need modeling clay, a knife, and a bowl of water. Take a large handful of clay and roll it into a thick cylinder. If the clay is too dry it will crumble, so dip your hands in water.

Stand the cylinder on its end and divide it into three equal sections by scratching rings into the surface. Then take the knife and carve your animal totems. Remember that your knife is sharp — make sure there is an adult to help you. Try to make your pole look good from the side and back, too! When you are happy with your design, allow it to dry overnight and then paint it.

Art materials

Artists today can choose from a huge variety of materials for their paintings and drawings. There are oil paints, acrylic paints, watercolors, and powder paints. Artists can use chalks, pastel colors, pencils, charcoal, felt-tip pens, or crayons. The thickness of paintbrushes ranges from broad to fine.

Some artists paint on a special fabric, called canvas. Canvas is best suited to acrylic and oil paints. There are also many kinds of paper on which to paint or draw. Paper can be thick or thin, smooth or rough, dull or glossy. The choice of paper depends on the kind of picture the artist wants. Pencil sketches look best on smooth paper, but chalks and pastels need a rougher surface. And you can buy a special paper for watercolor painting.

Do you recognize the art materials on these two pages? Which of them have you used? Some famous artists used only one or two types of materials in all their work. Others were equally good at using a range of materials. Try some of the projects in this book more than once, using different kinds of materials. Which work best for you?

Artists' biographies

A biography is the history of a person's life. These short biographies will help you to find out more about some of the artists mentioned in this book.

Albrecht Dürer (1471–1528)

The German artist Albrecht Dürer was a painter, engraver, and stained glass maker. He was also a jeweler. When he was only 13, he drew a skilled portrait of himself. This is recognized as the first European self-portrait. Dürer studied people and nature very closely and made thousands of drawings, paintings, and engravings of what he saw. Many people think that Dürer is one of the most talented artists who have ever lived.

Katsushika Hokusai (1760–1849)

The Japanese artist Hokusai made an astonishing number of drawings, prints, and paintings. From the age of six, he spent most of his time drawing. By the time he was 50, he had produced more pictures and designs than anybody could count. But he didn't paint or draw any of his famous pictures until he was over 65! His life was very disorganized. He changed his name 50 times. He moved 93 times. He moved when his house became too dirty to clean up! He

was always poor. Hokusai's works became popular when he was a very old man. His best-known pictures show different views of Mount Fuji.

Leonardo da Vinci (1452–1519)

Leonardo da Vinci lived in Italy at the beginning of a time of great changes. People were starting to recognize the importance of art, architecture, science, and literature. This period is called the Renaissance. Leonardo was a talented engineer, scientist, and mathematician, as well as a painter, sculptor, and architect. He studied the science of the human body and was the first painter to show people with realistic expressions in accurate positions. His best-known painting, the *Mona Lisa*, hangs in the Louvre, a famous art gallery and museum in Paris.

Henri Matisse (1869–1954)

The modern French artist Henri Matisse studied law before turning to painting. His pictures are full of decorative patterns of lines and colors. At the beginning of the 1900s, Matisse was the leader of a group of young painters who were known as Les Fauves. This means

The Wild Things. They were called this because of the way they enjoyed bright, powerful colors. They weren't interested in copying shapes from nature. Instead, they turned everything they saw into flat patterns. This style has influenced many modern painters. Matisse was crippled by illness for the last twenty years of his life, but he carried on painting until the day he died.

Henri Rousseau (1844–1910)

Henri Rousseau was a French customs officer whose favorite hobby was painting. He is sometimes known as Le Douanier, or "the Customs Man." He eventually gave up his job to paint full time. He painted exotic animals and tropical scenery, although he had probably never been out of France. He used plain colors and clear outlines, and his paintings are very simple. This style of painting is called naive. Naive painters learn to paint without a teacher.

Joseph Mallord William Turner (1775–1851)

The English painter JMW Turner was the son of a London barber. He began to earn his living by painting scenes of churches and towns when he was only 13. These pictures were popular.

Turner's style changed as he became more and more fascinated by light and movement in nature. The pictures we know best are full of swirling color and light. These paintings were so different from ones painted by other artists of his time that even his friends thought he was insane! When Turner was an old man he refused to show anybody his paintings because no one appreciated them.

INDEX

A
Aboriginal pictures   38, 39
acrylic paint   42
Allotments   12
American artist   15
animal patterns   16, 17
animal portraits   36, 37
The Arnolfini Marriage   29
art materials   42, 43
artists' biographies   44, 45
Audubon, John James *(1785–1851)*   15
Australian art   38, 39

B
*Balloon-flower with Other Plants and
    Cicada*   5
bark pictures   38, 39
Bewick, Thomas *(1753–1828)*   33
block printing   32, 33
butterflies   15

C
canvas   42–43
carpet page   16–17
carving   41
chalk   42
charcoal   42
cinnabar   10
clay   41
cochineal   11
collage   9, 20–21
Constable, John *(1776–1837)*   22
crayon   28, 38, 42–43

D
da Vinci, Leonardo *(1452–1519)*   35
de Morgan, William *(1839–1917)*   30
designs   16, 17, 30, 31
Dreaming   38
Dürer, Albrecht *(1471–1528)*   14, 44
Dutch artists   4, 12, 34

E
earth colors   10
Elephant   34
English artists   7, 22, 30, 36, 45
van Eyck, Jan *(died 1441)*   29

F
felt-tip pen   42–43
Flemish artist   29
flowers   4
French artists   18, 19, 21, 44–45
Friedrich, Caspar-David *(1774–1840)*   8
fruit   4

G
German artists   8, 14, 44
van Gogh, Vincent *(1853–1890)*   12
gouache   14
A Great White Heron   15

H
The Hare   14
Hasan, Abul *(died c.1600)*   13
Hoji, Matsumato *(c.1740–1800)*   32
Hokusai, Katsushika *(1760–1849)*   6, 44
The Hollow of the Deep Sea Wave   6
van Huysum, Jan *(1682–1749)*   4

I
icebergs   8
illuminated manuscripts   16, 17
Indian artists   13, 36
insects   4, 5
Italian artist   35, 44

J
Japanese artists   5, 6, 32, 44
Japanese prints   32

K
kangaroos 38–39
Klee, Paul *(1879–1940)* 23

L
lapis lazuli 10
lead, white 11
Leonardo da Vinci *(1452–1519)* 35, 44
Lindisfarne Gospels 16, 17

M
Mansur *(died c.1600)* 36
marble 24, 25
Matisse, Henri *(1869–1954)* 21, 44–45
monks 17
Morris, William *(1834–1896)* 30
mosaics 24, 25
Mount Fuji 6
movement 6, 7, 34, 35

N
nightingale 33
North American Indian art 40, 41

O
oil paint 42
orpiment 11

P
paint brushes 42–43
Park near L 23
pastel 42
patterns 16, 17, 19, 22, 23
pencil 42
pigments 10, 11
poisonous colors 11
Pompeii 24
powder paint 42–43
printing 23, 32, 33

R
Rembrandt van Rijn *(1606–1669)* 34
Rousseau, Henri *(1844–1910)* 18, 45

S
saffron 11
scratch drawing 38
shadows 5, 35
shape 20, 21, 22, 23
shells 11
Sketches of Cats 35
The Snail 21
Snowstorm: Steamboat off a Harbour's Mouth 7
Squirrels in a Chennar Tree 13
still-life 4, 5
Still-life with Fruit and Flowers 4
Strawberry Thief 30

T
texture 4, 26, 27, 28, 29
totem poles 40, 41
Tropical Storm with a Tiger 19
Turkey Cock 36
Turner, JMW *(1775–1851)* 7, 45

U
ultramarine 10
Utamaro, Kitagawa *(1754–1806)* 5

V
van Eyck, Jan *(died 1441)* 29
van Gogh, Vincent *(1853–1890)* 12
van Huysum, Jan *(1682–1749)* 4
vermilion 10
*View of Salisbury Cathedral from the Bishop's
    Grounds* 22

W
watercolor 14, 15
White Ram 36
wind and water 6–7
woad 11
woodcuts 32, 33
The Wreck of The Hope 8

The publishers would like to thank the following for permission to reproduce these works of art:

Fish Mosaic from the 1st Century AD; Dreaming, Aboriginal painting; by courtesy of the Ancient Art and Architecture Collection, London, UK. *Still-life with Fruit and Flowers* by Jan van Huysum, 1682-1749, in the National Gallery, London, UK; *Snowstorm: Steamboat off a Harbour's Mouth* by JMW Turner, 1775-1851, in the Tate Gallery, London, UK; *The Wreck of The Hope* by Caspar-David Friedrich, 1774-1840, in the Kunsthalle, Hamburg, Switzerland; *The Allotments* by Vincent van Gogh, 1853-90, in a private collection; *The Hare* by Albrecht Dürer, 1471-1528, in the Albertina Graphic Collection, Vienna, Austria; *View of Salisbury Cathedral from the Bishop's Grounds* by John Constable, 1776-1837, in the Victoria and Albert Museum, London, UK; *Park near L* by Paul Klee, 1879-1940, in the Kunstmuseum, Bern, Switzerland; *Nightingale* by Thomas Bewick, 1753-1828, owned by the Folio Society, London, UK; all by courtesy of the Bridgeman Art Library, London, UK. *Squirrels in a Chennar Tree* (EK 1647) by Abul Hasan; *Cross Carpet Page* (Cotton Nero C.IV, f210v) from the Lindisfarne Gospels, by courtesy of the British Library, London, UK. *Balloon-flower with Other Plants and Cicada* by Kitagawa Utamaro; *The Hollow of the Deep Sea Wave* by Hokusai; *Frog by Hoji*; *Elephant* by Rembrandt; all by courtesy of the Trustees of the British Museum, London, UK. *White Ram*, by courtesy of the Museum of English Naive Art, Bath, UK. *Tropical Storm with a Tiger* by Henri Rousseau; *The Arnolfini Marriage* by Jan van Eyck; both by courtesy of the Trustees, the National Gallery, London, UK. *A Great White Heron* by John James Audubon, by courtesy of the Natural History Museum, London, UK. *Sketches of Cats* by Leonardo da Vinci, by courtesy of Windsor Castle, UK, Royal Library, © HM The Queen. *The Snail* by Henri Matisse, by courtesy of the Tate Gallery, London, UK. Tile design by William de Morgan; *Strawberry Thief* by William Morris; *Turkey Cock* by Mansur; all by courtesy of the Board of Trustees of the Victoria & Albert Museum, London, UK. Aboriginal bark painting; North American totem pole; both by courtesy of the Werner Forman Archive, London, UK.

The publishers would like to give special thanks to staff at the Victoria & Albert Museum, London, and to Floyd Beckford and his colleagues at the British Museum, London.